DRAWING MYTHOLOGICAL MONSTERS

ILLUSTRATED BY JANOS JANTNER

PowerKiDS press™

New York

Published in 2013 by The Rosen Publishing Group, Inc.
29 East 21st Street, New York, NY 10010

First Edition

Produced for Rosen by Calcium Creative Ltd
Editors: Sarah Eason and Rosie Hankin
Editor for Rosen: Sara Antill
Book Design: Paul Myerscough

Illustrations by Janos Jantner

Library of Congress Cataloging-in-Publication Data

Jantner, Janos.
 Drawing mythological monsters / by Janos Jantner. — 1st ed.
    p. cm. — (How to draw monsters)
 Includes index.
 ISBN 978-1-4777-0309-0 (library binding) —
ISBN 978-1-4777-0340-3 (pbk.) — ISBN 978-1-4777-0341-0 (6-pack)
1. Animals, Mythical, in art—Juvenile literature. 2. Monsters in art—Juvenile
literature. 3. Drawing—Technique—Juvenile literature. I. Title.
 NC825.M9J36 2013
 743'.87—dc23

                                2012026335

Manufactured in the United States of America

CPSIA Compliance Information: Batch #W13PK7: For Further Information contact Rosen Publishing, New York, New York at 1-800-237-9932

CONTENTS

MONSTERS OF MYTH

From powerful dragons and terrible trolls to mysterious monsters such as Medusa, the Minotaur, and the Cyclopes, people have grown up with stories of magical beasts in myths and legends. Now you can bring your very own mythical creatures to life through art!

YOU WILL NEED

Just a few simple pieces of equipment are needed to create awesome monster drawings:

Sketchpad or paper
Visit an art store to buy good quality paper.

Pencils
A range of drawing pencils are essential. You will need both fine-tipped and thick-tipped pencils.

Eraser
You can remove any unwanted lines with an eraser, and you can even use it to add highlights.

Paintbrush, paints, and pens
Buy a set of quality paints, brushes, and coloring pens to add color to your monster drawings.

MONSTER FACTS

Once you've created your amazing mythical monsters, find out more about the creatures by checking out great monster facts!

HIDEOUS TROLL

This ugly creature comes from the myths of Scandinavia. Trolls were huge monsters that hid in caves deep beneath hills and mountains. They were also famous for lurking beneath bridges, where they waited for passing humans. When people crossed the bridge, the trolls ate them!

STEP 1

Draw rectangular shapes to create the troll's trunk and legs. Then use ovals for the head and arms. Draw a triangular shape for the club.

STEP 2

Draw over your shapes to create the troll's outline. Erase the shapes you drew in step 1. Draw rough lines for the face, hair, beard, hands, boots, clothes, and club.

STEP 3

Now you can begin to add more detail. Pencil lines to show strands of the creature's hair and beard. Add wrinkles and a snarling mouth to the face. Give the troll's tunic and pants ragged edges, and draw detail on the belt. Add muscle lines to its arms and fingernails to the hands. Finally, add sharp spikes to the troll's club.

STEP 4

Give your troll glaring eyes. Add more detail to its hair and beard. Add more muscle lines to the arms. Give the club a few rough edges. Then draw creases on the troll's clothes and belt to show its round belly.

STEP 5

Add more detail to the creature's skin, showing cuts, bruises, and rough edges. Then add shading beneath the troll's hair and clothes. This will help to give your drawing great depth and drama.

STEP 6.

Begin to color your creature. Use a palette of pink and gray for the skin. Paint the hair a red-brown color. Use gray for the belt and boots, and blue for the tunic. Color the monster's club brown.

STEP 7

Add white highlights to the beast's face, elbows, knuckles, club, and clothes. Use a dark gray paint to add more shadows to the skin, tunic, and boots. Use a deeper brown to add shade and depth to the club. Check that your troll has dirty hands, scaly skin, and gross fingernails!

MONSTER FACT!

It was very difficult to kill a troll. If a person knew the creature's name, they could destroy the creature. However, most heroes died trying to discover the wicked troll's name!

MONSTROUS MEDUSA

Medusa was a terrible creature with live snakes for hair! She was once a beautiful woman who lived where the Sun never shone. She asked a Greek goddess, Athena, if she could travel to see the Sun, but Athena refused. Medusa disobeyed Athena, so the angry goddess turned her into a monster.

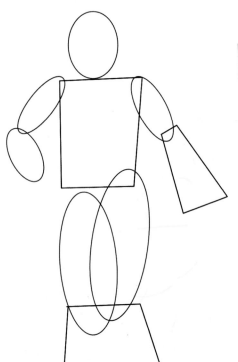

STEP 1

Draw rectangles for the trunk and skirt. Use ovals for the head, arms, and legs.

STEP 2

Draw the creature's outline, then erase the shape lines. Draw her face and the wriggling snakes. Add her flowing dress.

STEP 3

Now add muscle lines to Medusa's arms and neck. Add the detail of her collarbone. Draw her sharp, pointed fingernails and the claws on her feet. Draw her eyes and snarling mouth. Add wrinkles to her face. Now draw the creases of her long dress.

STEP 4

Medusa looks frightening already, but don't forget the slithering snakes on her head! Each one is as terrible as the next. Add detail to their beady eyes and forked tongues. Your monster looks hideous!

11

STEP 5

Now add detail to your creature's scaly skin. Add shading to her face, neck, arms, and feet. This will give your picture depth and make Medusa look even more frightening.

STEP 6

Color Medusa to make her stand out. Use a palette of pink and gray for her skin. Add bright red eyes! Color her dress a glowing orange-red. Use a blue-gray for the slithering snakes.

STEP 7

Complete your image by adding light cream highlights to Medusa's face, neck, arms, and feet. Add glints of reflected light to her razor-sharp nails. Highlight parts of the snakes, too. Give them green eyes and red tongues. Finally, add more shade and depth to Medusa's flowing dress.

MONSTER FACT!

Athena cursed Medusa so that any man she looked at would turn to stone. In Greek legend, the hero Perseus destroyed Medusa by safely looking at her in the reflection of his shield, then cutting off her head.

13

MIGHT OF THE MINOTAUR

The Minotaur was a horrible monster that lived in a maze on the Greek island of Crete. A half-man and half-bull monster, the Minotaur ate children that were sacrificed by the King of Crete.

STEP 1

Draw rectangles for the Minotaur's body, lower legs, and arms. Use ovals for the head, horns, and upper legs and arms.

STEP 2

Draw a finer pencil outline and erase the lines you drew in step 1. Add the ears, horns, hair, face, hands, hooves, and tail.

STEP 3

Begin to add detail to your Minotaur's body. Draw the outline of the nose, and add a nose ring. Add texture to the beast's mane. Pencil lines on the Minotaur's chest for its muscles and rib cage. Add fur to the top of the hooves. Then add the Minotaur's weapon, a sharp ax.

STEP 4

Add more features to the creature's face. Include its piercing eyes and terrible teeth. Draw lines of fur on the chest, back, legs, and tail. Add fingernails and knuckles to the hands.

Now add detail to the horns and ax. Add wrinkle lines to the face, and show the bulging muscles of the upper body. Shade parts of the Minotaur's face and body to add depth.

STEP 6

Paint your Minotaur using a palette of pink and brown. Now add light and shade to its skin and hair. Use a light cream for the horns and silver for the nose ring and ax head. Now your beast is really coming to life!

STEP 7

To finish your drawing, add white tints to the beast's eyes. Add highlights to its mane and fur, too. Don't forget the bulging muscles of its body. Some light tints on the nose ring will add depth. Try to make the ax blades look sharper, too. Don't forget to give the creature's gruesome teeth a brilliant sparkle!

MONSTER FACT!

The King of Crete did not sacrifice children from Crete. Instead, every year he sent for children from Athens to be the victims. One year, Theseus, the prince of Athens, offered to be a sacrifice in order to destroy the beast. Theseus traveled to Crete, where he killed the monstrous Minotaur.

LUCKY DRAGON

n Chinese legend, dragons were wise and powerful beasts. Dragons were symbols of luck and good fortune, and could help people to overcome evil. Dragons were ancient creatures that could live for hundreds or even thousands of years.

STEP 1

Draw ovals for the dragon's head and body. Draw a circle for its tail. Use rectangles and ovals for its legs. Then add the tip of the tail.

STEP 2

Draw a fine line over the outline and erase your rough shapes from step 1. Start to add the detail of your dragon's face and feet.

STEP 3

Add spines to your dragon's back, and sharp claws to its toes. Draw fine, feathery details around the gaping mouth, and a wispy end to the tail. Don't forget the nostrils and the beast's piercing eyes. The dragon is a powerful creature, and these details will make it look awesome.

STEP 4

Now add ridges to the beast's neck and belly. Give the face character and fill the mouth with sharp teeth. Add pencil lines to show the creature's powerful leg muscles.

19

STEP 5

Now get to work on the dragon's body. Add detail to the skin to make it look rough and scaly. Add shading beneath the chin and under the legs, too.

STEP 6

It's time to breathe some fire into your dragon! Use a palette of blue and green for the body. Use red and orange for the spines and details on the face. Then give the neck a red shimmer!

STEP 7

Use some white highlights to really bring the colors to life. Light tints will give the spines a sharper edge and will help make the eyes sparkle. Add highlights to the creature's body, too. This will make the skin look leathery and realistic.

MONSTER FACT!

In Chinese mythology there are nine dragons and each had a different power. Of the nine dragons, four were the most powerful and were the kings of all dragons

DEADLY SPHINX

A sphinx was a monster that often had the head of a woman, the body of a lion, the wings of an eagle, and a snake for a tail. This incredible-looking creature comes from ancient Egyptian mythology. The ancient Egyptians carved many statues of sphinxes that are still standing today.

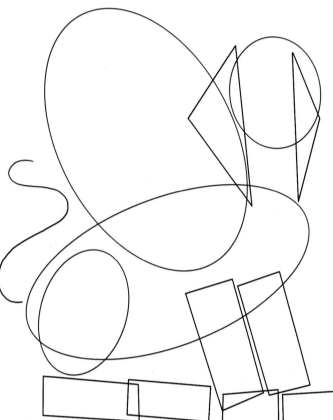

STEP 1

Draw ovals for the sphinx's head, wings, and body. Use rectangles for the front legs and feet. Draw triangles for the headdress.

STEP 2

Pencil the sphinx's outline, then erase the shape lines from step 1. Draw the face, feet, wings, and tail.

STEP 3

Now focus on the features of the face. Add large eyes and arched eyebrows. Add detail to the headdress and give the wings a feathery feel. Now draw the furry paws, revealing razor-sharp claws!

STEP 4

Don't forget to add a snake's head to the tail. Pencil lines will help to decorate the headdress. Give the wings some fuller feathers, too. Add futher lines to show the fur of the lion body and large, powerful muscles on the front and back legs.

STEP 5

By adding shading to the sphinx you will start to give the creature a 3D effect. Shade the hollows of the eye sockets, the area beneath the chin, and the wings and legs.

STEP 6

Use different colors to show each part of the sphinx. Use brown for the lion's body, green and blue for the snake, red, gold, and green for the eagle's wings, and pink for the woman's face. Color the headdress, too.

STEP 7

Now use light tints to give your creature further depth. White highlights on the body will give the lion's fur a soft sheen. Highlights will also bring out the detail of the face. Don't forget to tint the tail and the sharp fangs of the snake!

MONSTER FACT!

In ancient Egyptian legend, anyone who came across a sphinx was asked to solve a puzzle by the monster. If they could not answer the problem, they were killed by the sphinx. The puzzle was almost impossible to answer, but one hero named Oedipus solved it. In despair at losing the challenge, the sphinx threw itself off a mountainside and fell to its death.

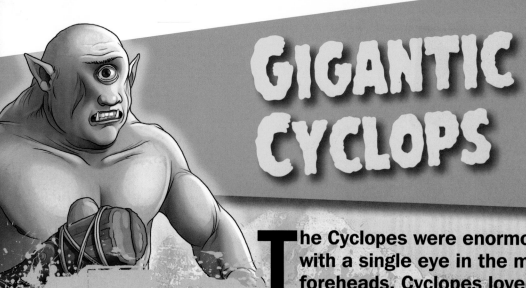

GIGANTIC CYCLOPS

The Cyclopes were enormous giants with a single eye in the middle of their foreheads. Cyclopes loved battles and fought each other all the time. Of all their victims, humans were their favorite food.

STEP 1

Draw triangles for the Cyclops's trunk and neck. Use ovals for its head and thighs. Draw rectangles for the arms, lower legs, and club.

STEP 2

Pencil the monster's outline, then erase the shape lines from step 1. Draw the eye, ears, hands, feet, and loincloth.

STEP 3

Now add a nose above the creature's snarling mouth. Draw toenails and fingernails and add detail to the beast's bulging muscles. Further define the heavy club in the Cyclops's hand. This is a deadly weapon!

STEP 4

Draw further detail to the creature's scary eye. Don't forget its terrible teeth. Add more detail to the ears, knees, and knuckles. Add some string to the club to hold the stone blade in place.

STEP 5

Now shade the legs, arms, hands, feet, neck, and upper body. Add shading to the eye socket to give it further definition. Pencil some more creases on the monster's loincloth.

STEP 6

Color your Cyclops with a dark pink palette for its skin. Use shading to define the powerful muscles. Add the club's brown wooden handle and gray stone blade. Give the hideous beast a green loincloth.

STEP 7

Finally, add pale highlights to the skin to add depth. Give the gruesome teeth a sparkle, and use a touch of white for the scary glint in the eye. Light tints will also add texture to the blade, handle of the club, and the folds of the loincloth. Don't forget to add a shiny tint to the ugly, bald head!

MONSTER FACT!

The most famous of the Cyclops giants was named Polyphemus. In legend, the Greek hero Odysseus killed Polyphemus by first drugging the monster with wine, and then spearing its single eye.

GLOSSARY

ancient (AYN-shent) Very old, from a long time ago.

Athena (uh-THEE-nuh) The Greek goddess of wisdom.

Athens (A-thenz) The capital of Greece.

challenge (CHA-lenj) A very difficult task.

club (KLUB) A heavy stick used as a weapon.

cursed (KURSD) Put a spell on someone to give him bad luck.

detail (dih-TAYL) The fine pencil markings on a drawing.

disobeyed (dis-oh-BAYD) Went against someone's orders.

drama (DRAH-muh) Excitement and exciting events.

drugging (DRUG-ing) Giving someone drugs or alcohol.

fangs (FANGZ) Long, sharp teeth.

goddess (GAH-des) A female god.

Greek (GREEK) A person or something from Greece.

highlights (HY-lytz) Light parts.

legend (LEH-jend) A very old story.

loincloth (LOYN-kloth) A piece of cloth, worn around the waist.

mane (MAYN) Long hair around the neck of a lion or other creature.

maze (MAYZ) A pattern of narrow paths, with one path leading to the center of the maze.

mythical (MITH-ih-kul) From old, famous stories called myths.

myths (MITHS) Very famous, ancient stories.

nostrils (NOS-trulz) Openings in the head through which an animal breathes.

palette (PA-lit) A range of colors.

ragged (RAG-ed) Rough, uneven.

reflection (rih-FLEK-shun) A picture of something or someone in a mirror or polished surface.

sacrificed (SA-kruh-fysd) Killed to keep a god or monster happy.

Scandinavia (skan-dih-NAY-vee-uh) Northern Europe, usually Norway, Sweden, and Denmark.

shading (SHAYD-ing) Pencil lines that add depth to a picture.

shield (SHEELD) A large metal or wooden object used by a warrior to protect themselves in battle.

symbols (SIM-bulz) Signs.

tunic (TOO-nik) A dress-like garment that falls to the knee.

victims (VIK-timz) People who are killed, injured, or harmed in some way.

FURTHER READING

Bingham, Jane. *Chinese Myths*. Myths From Many Lands. New York: Windmill Books, 2009.

Ganeri, Anita, and David West. *Creatures of Myths and Legends*. Monster Fight Club. New York: PowerKids Press, 2012.

Green, Jen. *Ancient Greek Myths*. Myths from Around the World. New York: Gareth Stevens, 2010.

WEBSITES

Due to the changing nature of Internet links, PowerKids Press has developed an online list of websites related to the subject of this book. This site is updated regularly. Please use this link to access the list: www.powerkidslinks.com/htdm/myth/

INDEX